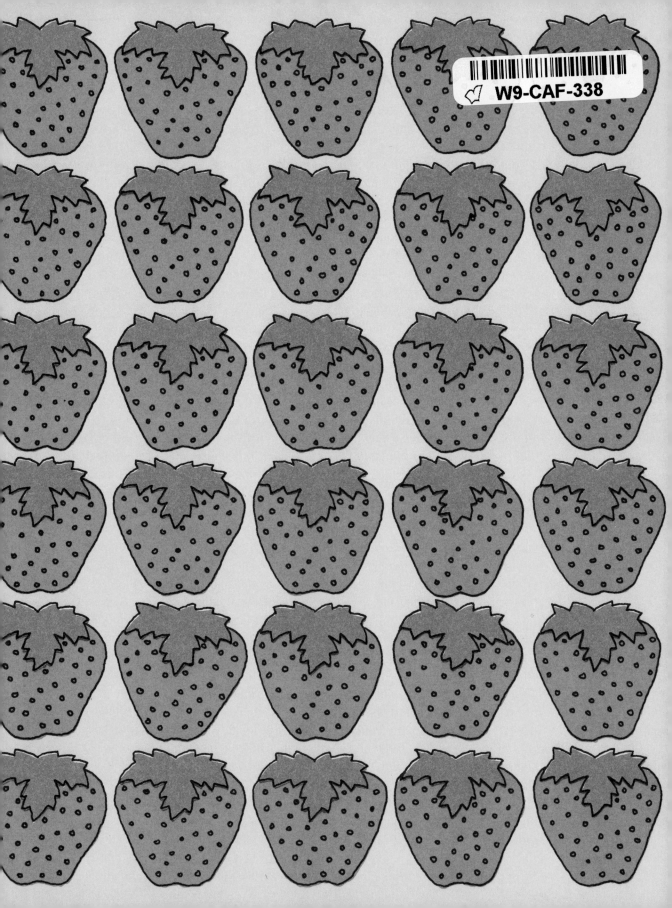

this
strawberry book
belongs to

Megan
Cook

*this book
is for
Kathy
and
Bonnie
and
Joyce
also
William*

Copyright © 1975 by One Strawberry, Inc.
All rights reserved
Printed in the United States of America
Library of Congress Catalog Card Number: 75-12150
ISBN: Trade 0-88470-018-6, Library 0-88470-019-4
strawberry books • distributed by Larousse & Co., Inc.
572 Fifth Avenue, New York, N.Y. 10036

Weekly Reader Books Edition

yes
and
no

a book of
opposites
by Richard Hefter

a strawberry book™

a strawberry book®

pull · push

Pulling an elephant.

Pushing an elephant.

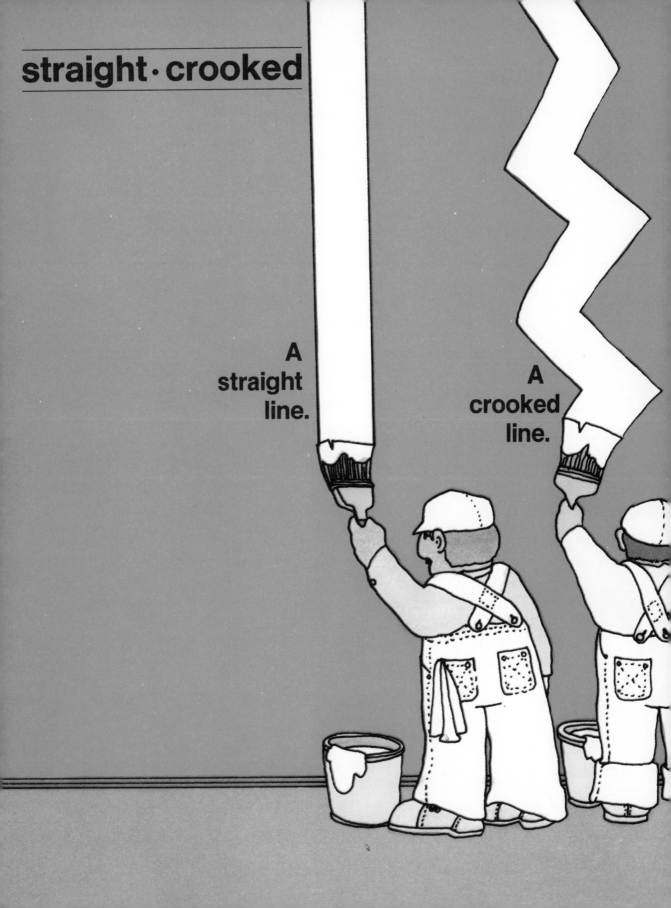

**high · low
up · down
hill · valley**

High up
on a hill.

Low down
in a valley.

smooth · rough

The car is on a smooth road.
The jeep is on a rough road.

inside · outside

Right side up. Upside down.

Inside a box.

Outside a box.

big · little

A big balloon.

A little balloon.

above · below

An elephant below the table.

An elephant above the table.

The bear on the left is neat.
The bear on the right is messy.

tall · short
front · back

Two tall bears in front.
Two short bears in back.
One short bear's back.

Marvin is fat, his jacket is tight.
Harold is thin, his jacket is loose.

over · under

A dog, over a cat, over a goat, over a kangaroo.

A kangaroo, under a goat, under a cat, under a dog.

The lamp is off, it is dark.

The lamp is on, it is light.

in · out
come · go
hello · goodbye

hello

Alligators come in.

goodbye

Alligators go out.

asleep · awake
soft · hard

This bed is soft.
This bear is asleep.

This bed is hard.
This bear is awake.

This bear has hot soup.

This bear has cold soup.

winter · summer
cold · warm
cloudy · sunny

A cold and cloudy winter day.

A warm and sunny summer day.

sweet · sour

Honey is sweet.

Lemons are sour.

shout · whisper

WHISPER · ·

SHOUT!

lost · found

He lost his shoe.

She found it.

un makes lots of things into opposites.

happy — unhappy

tied — untied

bent — unbent

dressed — undressed

finished — unfinished